Contents

Any words appearing in the text in bold, **like this**, are explained in the glossary.

Information in our world

 How many different **sources** of information can you see here?

You are surrounded by information. Information is what people know about things. It includes photographs, signs, **symbols**, sounds, and words that tell you how to do things or where to go.

In your everyday life you often need to find certain types of information. You might need information for a school project or about a new hobby. This book will help you find what you need.

At school, you sometimes need to work on group projects.

Questions

One of the quickest ways to find information is to ask questions. First, decide who will know the answer. Then, think about how to word your question. Sometimes you will need to ask or answer more questions after you get an answer.

 Make sure that you stay safe. Only ask a stranger for help if you are with an adult.

Be polite and listen carefully when you ask for information. The person you ask may suggest that you talk to another person or look at printed information.

 Can you think of a clearer question for this boy to ask?

Printed information

 Libraries are great places to find all sorts of information.

Printed information comes in many forms including books and newspapers. There are two types of books: fiction and **non-fiction**. Story books are fiction. Non-fiction books, such as encyclopedias and dictionaries, give you facts rather than stories.

In a library, ask a librarian or use a catalogue to find the information you are looking for. A librarian can help you find a book using the **Dewey Decimal System**. You can also use an **online catalogue** that lists information **sources** found in the library.

 To find a book in a library, you need to follow a special system. A librarian can help you to understand this system.

Useful features

 Use the features of a book to help you find the information you want.

Once you have found the book that you want, there are **features** inside it that will help you to find the exact information you need. A table of contents lists the headings for each page of the book. Look at the table of contents in this book for an example.

An index gives an alphabetical list of subjects to be found within the book. Entries in encyclopedias and dictionaries are also alphabetical.

It is much easier to look for a particular topic when the entries are arranged in alphabetical order.

Organizing information

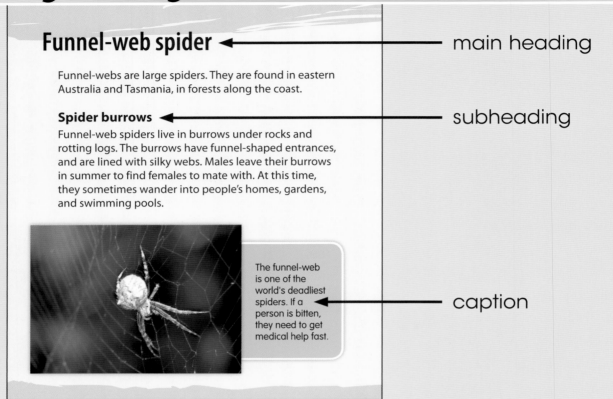

Funnel-web spider ← main heading

Funnel-webs are large spiders. They are found in eastern Australia and Tasmania, in forests along the coast.

Spider burrows ← subheading

Funnel-web spiders live in burrows under rocks and rotting logs. The burrows have funnel-shaped entrances, and are lined with silky webs. Males leave their burrows in summer to find females to mate with. At this time, they sometimes wander into people's homes, gardens, and swimming pools.

The funnel-web is one of the world's deadliest spiders. If a person is bitten, they need to get medical help fast. ← caption

The main heading on a page tells you what kind of information is on that page. Smaller text is used for **subheadings**. Subheadings tell you what type of information is in the next paragraph. Captions describe what appears in a photograph or artwork. They usually give information that cannot be found in the main text.

In **non-fiction** books there is often a **glossary**. This is an alphabetical list of words that may be difficult to understand or need further explanation. Words that can be found in the glossary are usually shown in bold lettering in the main text.

Glossary

database way of storing and organizing information

features characteristics or appearance of an object

graphic organizer way of showing information in a chart, table, or graph

keyword word that describes the particular subject you want to find information about

menu offers a list of subjects included as web pages on a website. The menu of a website is like a table of contents. If you choose one of the things on the list, you can jump to that subject.

non-fiction text that is factual rather than made up like in a story

online connected to the Internet

online catalogue electronic list of all the information sources, such as books, films, and magazines, that can be found in a particular library. The list can be accessed by computer.

podcast recorded programme of talk or music that can be taken off the Internet and listened to at any time

reliable trustworthy

search engine website that provides lists of other websites about a particular subject

source place in which we can find things such as information. Books, magazines, and the Internet are all sources of information.

symbol word or picture that stands for something else. For example, a triangle made up of three arrows is the sign for recycling.

web name given to the interconnected websites on the Internet. The web is similar to a spider web. Like a spider web, the websites are connected.

web browser program on your computer that allows you to view websites

web page term used to describe one page of a website. A website is often made up of many web pages. The main or starting page of a website is called the home page.

wiki website that allows many people to add or change information

30

Graphic organizers

Information does not just have to appear as words and photographs. **Graphic organizers** can also be very helpful. Sometimes looking at information in a graph, table, or chart makes it much easier to understand.

 This is called a line graph. It shows how things change over time.

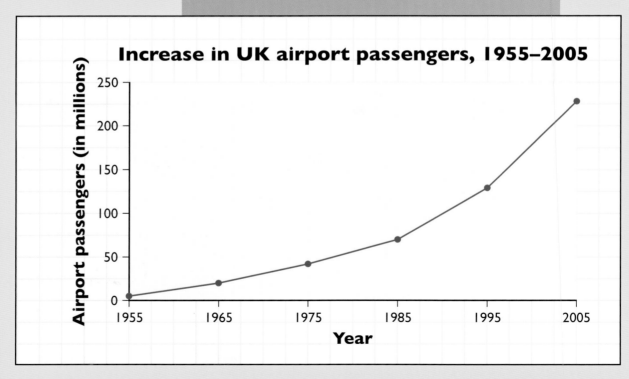

Increase in UK airport passengers, 1955–2005

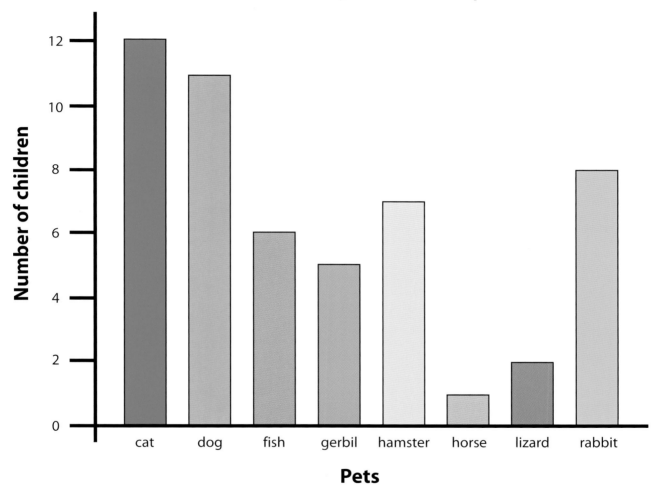

Number of children in Banbury School who own pets

 This is called a bar graph. It shows how much of something there is.

Electronic information

Electronic information includes **databases**, **online** encyclopedias and dictionaries, DVDs, websites, **wikis**, and **podcasts**.

TIC Travel Information Centre

Home | Search | Our Collection | Thesaurus | About Us | My TIC

Search TIC Collection

Search Term(s): [   ]

» Advancd Search
» Thesaurus
» Help

Search in: [🔍]

Search

Records added in the last month: **3278**

A database is a collection of information stored electronically. To find information in a database you will need to search using **keywords**.

Podcasts can be listened to at any time on your computer or an MP3 player. They cover a wide range of topics. You can either sign up to receive new episodes as soon as they are available or click on them one by one.

 You can listen to a podcast or view a video online.

The Internet

The Internet. links together computers all over the world. This means people can view information stored or created on other computers. Information on the Internet includes websites, encyclopedias, newspapers, email, **wikis**, and social networks. You can use email to contact people anywhere.

Most information on the Internet can be found on websites. Websites can be set up by governments, organizations, or ordinary people.

Not all information on the Internet is good or **reliable**. You should check with an adult before using a new Internet site.

Searching the Internet

The best way to look up information is to use a **search engine**. A search engine looks through all the websites on the Internet to find the ones that you might find helpful. It is a good idea to use **keywords** when you search the Internet. These are words that describe the subject you want to find out about.

Search web

| elephants | **GO** |

Keywords are useful because they help narrow down your search.

A shorter list of websites is more helpful in answering your question.

If you type in several keywords rather than just one, the search engine provides a much shorter list of websites.

Websites

There are millions of websites on the Internet. Websites usually have a number of separate pages within them. These pages, called **web pages**, can include text, pictures, sound, and video.

 Some websites are made especially for children. Others may have a special section for children.

You can go to different parts of a website by clicking on the **menu**. This is found on the home page, which is usually the opening page of a website. Sometimes the menu is found on every page of the website.

menu

 Menus are usually found at the top or at the left side of a web page.

Beware!

 If a website looks strange to you, or if you cannot find out who the author or creator of the **web page** is, ask an adult for help.

Not all websites contain **reliable** information. Remember, anyone can put together a website. It is a good idea to look at the websites of well-known organizations such as museums, the BBC, or NASA.

When you look at a website, you have to
be careful what you click on. Some websites
include adverts. Adverts try to sell things
to people who use the website. Be careful
about the information you find on sites
with adverts.

What's next?

There is a lot of information available and it can sometimes be difficult to find what you want. Asking questions, looking at books, and searching the Internet are just some of the ways you can find new information.

 Stay on top of all the information you have found by being organized.

 Sometimes it helps to talk things through with a friend.

Once you have looked at many different **sources** of information, you then need to sort it out. You need to choose which bits are the most useful and most **reliable** for what you want to do.

Activities

Practice makes perfect

Practise what you have learned in this book. Search for information about a musical instrument on the Internet using **keywords**. Before you begin, think about the question you wish to answer.

- Do you want to know the different types of instrument?

- Do you want to know about one type of instrument?

Use keywords that will best help you find the information you are looking for. Gradually change or add to the keywords to narrow down your search. For example, you might decide to narrow your search to a bass electric guitar.

Always ask for help if you need it.

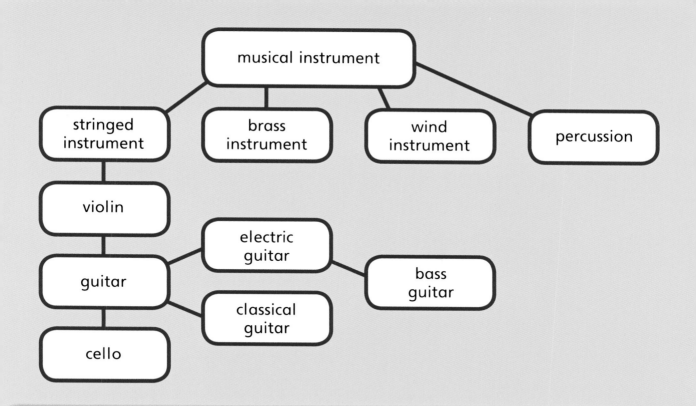

Fake websites – How good are your detective skills?

You should not believe everything you see or read on the Internet. Make a list of things that tell you that these are fake or bogus websites:

- Does the Jackalope exist? Look at the website www.sudftw.com/jackcon.
- Do you believe that there is a real dog island? (www.thedogisland.com/)
- Do you believe that there is a tree octopus? (http://zapatopi.net/treeoctopus/)

Glossary

database way of storing and organizing information

Dewey Decimal System number system that libraries use to organize books on the shelves

features characteristics or appearance of an object

glossary alphabetical list that explains difficult words

graphic organizer way of showing information in a chart, table, or graph

keyword word that describes the particular subject you want to find information about

menu offers a list of subjects included as web pages on a website. The menu of a website is like a table of contents. If you choose one of the things on the list, you can jump to that subject.

non-fiction text that is factual rather than made up like in a story

online connected to the Internet

online catalogue electronic list of all the information sources, such as books, films, and magazines, that can be found in a particular library. The list can be accessed by computer.

podcast recorded programme of talk or music that can be taken off the Internet and listened to at any time

reliable trustworthy

search engine website that provides lists of other websites about a particular subject

source place in which we can find information. Books, magazines, and the Internet are all sources of information.

subheading paragraph heading

symbol word or picture that stands for something else. For example, a triangle made up of three arrows is the sign for recycling.

web page term used to describe one page of a website. A website is often made up of many web pages. The main or starting page of a website is called the home page.

wiki website that allows many people to add or change information

Find out more

Books

My First Email Guide, Chris Oxlade (Heinemann Library, 2007)

My First Internet Guide, Chris Oxlade (Heinemann Library, 2007)

Websites

KidsClick – Searching the Internet

www.kidsclick.org/wows/

Searching the Internet to find information requires some skills. KidsClick is a great place to learn searching lessons. Have fun working your way through the nine worlds of information.

CBBC Newsround

www.bbc.co.uk/cbbc/help/safesurfing

This BBC website gives you advice on staying safe while you are on the Internet.

Yahoo! Kids – Homework Help

http://kids.yahoo.com/learn

This website includes links to an encyclopedia, dictionary, maps, and lots of other useful websites.

Ask Kids – Schoolhouse

www.askkids.com/schoolhouse?pch=sch

Ask Kids is a great search engine specially created for use by children.

Index